D1617513

# SWEETCLOVER

## Other Books by Shann Ray

*Balefire*
*American Masculine*
*Atomic Theory 432*
*Forgiveness and Power in the Age of Atrocity*
*American Copper*
*Blood Fire Vapor Smoke*

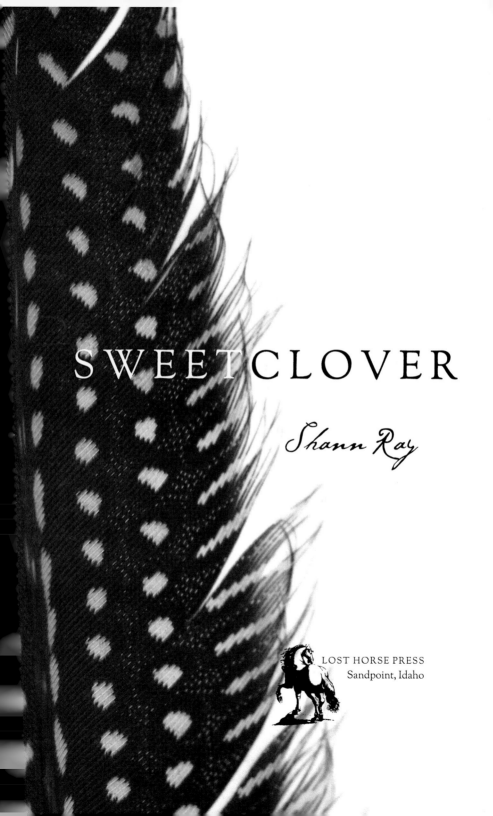

# SWEETCLOVER

*Shann Ray*

LOST HORSE PRESS
Sandpoint, Idaho

*Author Photo:* Vanessa Kay.
*Book & Cover Design:* Christine Holbert.

FIRST EDITION

*This and other fine Lost Horse Press titles may be viewed online at www.losthorsepress.org.*

LIBRARY OF CONGRESS CATALOGUING-IN-PUBLICATION DATA
is available from the Library of Congress.

ISBN 978-0-9991994-5-9

*for Jennifer*

# Table of Contents

## I LUPINE

# II DARK HORSE BRIGHT FIELD

# III WILD ROSE

Wild nights—Wild nights!

—*Emily Dickinson*

# I
Lupine

## Ecstasy

In the dark of morning,
the way flesh
encompasses bone
is nearly visible again
but when the day is full,
its skeleton laid bare
at the foot of this bright
mountain speaks my name
saying, remember

these tines of horn
like fingers,
the crown rack of bull elk
and the white bone skull,
leg bones scattered, fanned
to vanishing,
the body cage blown
back and ribwork emptied to echo

the crescent moon
seeking conference with God.
The way she looks at me
over the kitchen table
reminds me how
last night she kissed me
without spareness or greed,
but with a violence

akin to the sound
I heard rounding a tarn
of the west Beartooths
at dawn,
a melody of bugles
turning my face to the sky
where stars failed
and night gave way
to the sun.

## Vernal

Not any woman or any woman's body,
only her angled bones and swivel
show I am not bent to love.
But she sheds my ill will
anyway and removes her clothes. I am

the river, the mountain, she says,
beargrass and ladyslipper, lupine, paintbrush.
She waits
to make me face my pride, the old
worn boots in my farmer's field,
my feet of clay, the trace
    of generations of women-hating men
    like lead in my blood, times one, times ten.


2

Love defines
then speaks
to wake the
hands withheld and body shaken,
finding my heart on foreign soil
and you in the distance
you loved me in,
burnt sun of the evening star,
your thin collarbones like liminal scars,
bite of dusk on the mountain rim, and
Venus in your mortal cry.

## Devil's Slide Near Gardner

As a boy in Montana
I never thought I'd
curse a woman
but here I am,
a man
standing near the door
and screaming at you like a fool.

I'm just home
from a long passage, the moon
silvering stones
along the riverbed south
of the window where I know you will
    sleep off the shame we brewed,
      waiting to eat our forgiveness again like food.

## Poem Against Poverty of Narrative

In the good light
of morning,
a gold lustrous
smoothing to the skin,
I'm reminded how, living
on the high desert, I ascribe to others the grit
I taste in my own teeth

and think I have the right
to blame. I blame God, especially,
whom I believe
deserves it most. Blame the parents also
and brothers and sisters of my enemy, over whom I claim
violence in my heart and with my hands

until I marry one of them.

*Radiance, Paradise Valley,*
*the Absaroka-Beartooth Wilderness, Montana*

I'm often blind but know
stars fire the indiscernible void and you
are in my arms again
and the day of jubilee begins.
Arise, shine, for your light has come
and the glory of the Lord
has arisen upon you.

Now we live, you say, as if in the bedchamber
of those freed from war. Like flowers when the sun wakes.

Everything
grows still. The jump and shout, the luminous turn,
the whisper, the winnowing, the infinite burn. Everything
tells me love endures.

## Mountain Homecoming

We hadn't seen each other
for days,
but when I came through
the door
her smile
changed me from one
who passes through this world
to one who falls
into his wife's arms and rests
his head against her shoulder and feels
when they lie down together her warm heart
beating against his chest,
    her hands hungry for his holding,
    his hands alive to her happiness.

## Late July, Great Falls, Montana

*Tongue in Groove* 1

The method still used
in superior craft flooring.
Along one edge
a slit opposite
a thin deep ridge
so that
with tongue in groove
the two are one
just as falls step down
into water
and mountains join
sky, the two no longer two

      but a
    single solid thing.

*Tongue in Groove 2*

A shaper is needed
to bring stone to life
like the wood shaper
in fine cabinetry.

Also common hand planes
by which the beloved holds
the hipbones of the beloved
and proceeds discovering

in wilderness or war
a plough plane for the groove
and a tongue plane for the tongue.
Just as you hold the back of my head

in your hands
for the most suitable ascension.

## At the Big Blackfoot River

Her lips set
to clear water,
she drinks
then lifts her head to fields
bent by wind, and
trees dead cut white
rooted below the waterline.

Tree bone
arched over a plateau
of blue camas
from here
to the mountain. For all
that is fallow, for all
that precedes bloom

her rope tone arms covenant with
her body
against me until she draws back
and I lose our days

festering
as she fathers me
preparing before me
a table
in the wilderness
so that I forget myself and
remember her rightly again.

## Pine Creek Falls, Below the Beartooth Highway

Hazel eye of animal, root stone
and vermillion, peeling birch, white aspen,
black pine near the treeline granite
and wolves in the deep quiet
running range to range—
we greet one another in the evening
and cross the plateau. Emigrant Peak
and Silver Gate, Tumble Peak and
Red Lodge and north to Heart Butte.
I breathe.
          Your autumn light.

## Hesperus

My four-year-old daughter handed me a card.
*To Daddy* written on the front
and inside a rough field
of five-pointed lights, and the words
*You're my favorite Daddy in the stars.*

In this western night we light the sky
like Vega, Deneb, Altair, Albireo,
the Summer Triangle,
Cygnus the Swan, our hair
tangled with wood and gravel,
our eyes like vacant docks
that beckon every boat.

*Tell me about the word
stars,* I said.

*Oh,* she said. *Sorry.
I didn't know
how to spell world.*

## Three Forks, Montana, Headwaters of the Missouri

On a cutbank over clear water
we admit to one another
we've considered others.
Late humbled, quiet
as our wedding rings.

Strengthen us
to wrestle the angel,
we implore.
In August a Montana river's best virtue
is clarity. I have found myself to be
impure: to walk upright
I must reset my bones and
       taste salt on my lips,
       soot beneath my tongue.

## Sunrift Gorge, Glacier National Park, Montana

*Wife Psalm 1*

Today you told me with your hand
holding mine, our legs interwoven,

your red patent heels
like small lacquered ships,

God will shout for joy.
The Lord God will be quiet

with love. God will cry out
with delight. And here I believed

this life is made
of mountain ranges and rivers!

Glacier Lily. Beargrass.
More. You make

every woman live.
I see them in you.

*Wife Psalm 2*

I hope I believe always
what you've said

of God. The knife in your hand
over the pears

at breakfast,
*Anima Christi,*

the feminine
soul of Christ

your bone-weary anthem
in our soft bed,

your cry
a God-bearing

cry. Your body
a banner over me.

*Wife Psalm 3*

Jennifer, on the mountain
or in our jon boat on the river

we agree Emily Dickinson's
women are not subdued or enslaved

by marriage. We have been enslaved
but we burn anyway, so when we die

our caskets will be covered in violets.
Hope, you say,

I want to bind myself to you

in this river,
to feel your life in every breath, your

      emily-whisper,
      love is stronger than death.

## Down From Beartooth Pass

Along the silver Yellowstone
in Lamar's valley of wolves
we walk at first light,
pausing near a shed buffalo horn
and finding farther on the black-white
feather of a scavenger bird.
At the river's edge, the bend of it
robin's egg blue, I think of you
saying we couldn't be
more than we were
last night
      where dusk settled like ash
      on the edge of the mountain.

## On Gunsight Mountain

I

I put my face to the ground.
God help me
eye the dead socket
of the eye, not turn
from the dark
hunger

still attached to the beak line
and below not a body but grey
rock. A hand-length lower,
the spidery foot, no lung cavity,
no tibia, no femur,
only a zygomatic arch and a gap
above a three-taloned grip
alone on the
earth forever.

## II

She wasn't so familiar
with sin, my wife,
until she met me
and then it became
as close as skin.
In the middle years
we watched night flourish,
the windows closed and the oven hot,

her hands on the table, her face
flinted with such wounding
I hated my life
and looked to the mountain
for what takes wing
and gives flight
and what goes on to surrender.

## Don't Fall

You don't have to
disfigure your face
to please me.
Help me. Stop me
so I can listen. Wife make me
lower my hands. Drive wedgewood in

and break me open
to receive you, blossoming
as we touch index
finger to forehead, breastbone, shoulder bones.
     Grip me like a crown.
     Lift your body. Lift your body down.

## How the Husband Understands the Wife's Body

From eyes to jaw
down the neck and over the apex

of her upraised torso
adored exalted
the S line arched backbent and beveled

concave into the musculature of stomach
to the pelvic anthem

and the slipstream
doublesphere that leads

to her thighs
and the lean composition

of legs and feet.
Whose feet
are beautiful
as the beloved's?

When you wake day speak night, robed in praise
or only light, I want to know you more.

## *Three Oceans Plateau,*
## *Beartooth Range, Montana*

We have come together
in late evening
through grace and strength
of mind, our loyal bodies dark
and deep. O Lord, we come fully awake
and we tremble. With your hands you
adore what we adore. When you shout
you cherish what we make. We won't resist
the turn of evening
nor weft of wing nor hawk's cry
nor the tunneling roar of the engines.
     If we die tonight, if the end comes, we die.

## Poem for All Who Doubting, Believe

Placing my palm on the lower back
of my wife, precisely in
the indentation the spine makes
where her muscles descend above
the most exquisite double rise,

the heart-shaped ascent of what
she has me call my own here
in mountain country
where she sits on the edge of a wooden bench

I feel the hum of her voice
at home in my hands.

## Fire of the Body

is not unlike
the planets and stars
over the high mountain plateau
north of Sleeping Giant.
Or Hesperus in her
evening gown.
Say the Swan's cross
on the rise toward the zenith
of a far and precise darkness—

        or in the morning
        in the kindness of our bed,
        your body
        tipped back, gilded
        like a struck match.

# II

Dark Horse Bright Field

*i* _____


Woodland-star
melody of evening
from the apple
of your mouth,
mornings the hush of blue-
capped tree swallows
angle
through the house,
through the words you make
of love
and a woman's
art. The day you die
       God sets an anvil
       in my heart.

I will cloak you like the sun

you say,
my robe a raiment radiance alight
my body ghostpipe    yours    night.

*iii*

Between you and me and the evening
there is the press of your hands
into my shoulders and the arrowleaf tilt
of your torso, the torque
of your hips,
the end
of despair in the neck hollow.

Moor yourself in me
tonight without fear.
Friendship
in this house and body
leans into
your polished chimes,
let the oil of gladness
burnish your paleborn skin
and blossoms blossom again.

*v* _____

Dear one,
did you marry
a devil's snare fool
who needs
more forgiveness
than Emily's editor?

Yes, you answer, and no—
not that much
forgiveness, but some—
some. Listen, you say—
mercy rests
in a blood-red chair.

When I wake
in your arms, I whisper,
forgive me,

committing again, as you
turn and take me
which makes us both more

sad and lonely,
but wood lily lovely
in our way.

*vii*

In the honest light
of the bathroom
refracted like water
revealing
every line and scar—the hard
curve of your ribs and arms,
of hollowed bell
and fluted vase,
the lift of your eyes,
your face
so adamant,
your open neck
flushed, hoping.

I love you like the cherry tree loves
its flowering, and waits
the whole year through, beset
with silence and naked cold,
content with winter's forging
from hard soil
miracles,
the color that flies and blankets the ground.

*ix*

We died together—
you and I under the dogwood
when we were
young and cut ditches
in our palms
and pressed our hands together
letting blood and water mix.

*x* _____

I have loved you many years now,
more years than
before I knew you,
and this pleases me,
all the bluebottle sweet-talk
days of you, knowing
you are with me and beyond me too.

*xi*

In the morning the arch
of your back is something
sculpted by light, mountain lily
off-white unadorned.
Higher the scapula a bone hinge
to your arms angled like wings
over a calm
shout across the chasm.

You tell me to wake you after an hour
of sleep, so we can go on living
and dying like the clothes we once wore.
Your windflower blouse,
pink bra with Spanish blackwork inlay, fitted skirt,
my shirt, tie, slacks, wingtips, your silk underwear,
silver heels and stockings.
Still life of us, but not us, all over the floor.

*xiii*
_____

(sugarbowl)

The door into you
is slick, so much
more slick than I imagined,
until I knew you.

*xiv*

Your angular bones
and the curved ones,
your forearms,
ghost flower flutter of your hands,
occipital and orbital bones
and pelvic crown tipped
to the small of your back.  I believe in these.

(blue virginsbower)

For so long we weren't scared
when we were naked together

but now
we are afraid again.

(purple boneset)

When from the stand of cottonwoods
small white birds floated
over the big-bodied river at dusk,
I knew I loved you.
From the bands of muscle on your
arms and down your shoulder blades
to the feathered double-reed of your
lower back. Your trim lateral
lines, your strength,
your laughter
take me to forbidden places.
To a woman's knowledge.

In the black night
sex pushed the heels of your hands
into my chest and made you
glow like a burning house.

You set my head in your lap when it was over
and spoke my name until we slept,
and then in sleep I saw your
red-winged blackbirds along the fence line
of our dreams.

Am I worthy of loving
you? I ask
and you look up
then go back to the task
of night, dreaming.

So I persist, Let me count
the ways. But you are silent.

Only later when I
touch your cheekbone
in the pitch dark
do you seize my wrist
and come fully awake—
peering into my eyes to say
God has clothed us in splendor.

*xx*

In your sweetclover kiss
I know
the most generous part of this world.

*xxi*

When you speak
of my various and specific
faults, my jaw hurts.
I see the nightshade
years of work ahead.
Don't fret, you say,
your hand on the back of my head,
we have today.

III Wild Rose

## This Body

You are
the threshold
of stars, beloved,

a field of lights
in the house of the sky.
The way you see me

and take me to you
is sanctuary,
refuge,
river.

## June 2ⁿᵈ, 1990

In the winter thaw
of this God-given grace

I find the warmth of your face
on the cool of mine.

With touch and dismissal and gestures
we knock down the doors, we satiate.

Do we have to undress in order to feel
the eye of spring and the lovely wheel?

The war we make of supremacy
ascends in you, ascends in me.

Lay down your arms in disarray
O sister my sister my light of day

    I shudder at how boldly we fall
    yet return to be kissed, to be given away.

## Montana Waterways

When we came into
our own in our thirties
we hoped we would have decades yet
of great good loving. The music
of your clavicle. Your little death kiss.
Enough wetness
to cover the continent,
but hearing you whisper,
your lips touching the bone
behind my ear,
I noticed the black oil crows
perched on our shoulders.

## When Lightning Falls in Love with Deep Pockets

What would you like me to do
to you? you asked
in the middle
of our bed,
the storm gunmetal black
and your nakedness
against the window
a weather vane
God made.

## Montana Nude and Beautiful

O Beautiful your honey thighs
find rest

like amber waves of grain.
Your ample mountain majesties rise
above the fruited plain.

O Beautiful my Beautiful
God sheds his grace on thee
and crowns my good with sisterhood
from sea to shining sea.

O Beautiful in living dreams
we see your sparkling towers,

your alabaster city's gleam, the wonder
of your powers.

O my, Beautiful, you confirm our souls
in self-control, unfurl our nights, fill our days

with *E pluribus unum*. In bed we are saved.
Beautiful before you go, O don't let us waiver:
the land of the free, O come let us savor.

## Alpenglow Music Box

When mountain men descend
the last ridge through pine
and black hawthorn into the dark
fields, and when they lay up their boots,
I am still one of them
in the high wire symphony

of the city where I turn the lights low
and cross myself at the office door,
before stumbling road over road
back to you. At day's end
in a darkness so black I can't see
my hands, you welcome me with joy.

# In Morning Light

*for Isabella*

Over a simple blue
bowl and spoon
my young Isabella, only five,
eats oatmeal.

The soft dark
wood of the kitchen table
offsets her skin, and
her eyes astonish me
as she chews.

So mundane
the mandible,
the jawline and light
brow just
like her mother's.
Why do I love you

so much? I ask,
but she ignores me. Why
do I love you so much?
I ask again. Hmmm,
she hums.

Why? Her serious eyes and voice say,
"God made you to love me."

## Mountain Body Frisson

1

Apparently it is not the torque
but the gravity
that matters. That, and the strength
or slickness of the channel.

2

The greater the gravity
the higher the voltage attained,
the greater the slickness
the more nothing remains
the same. Who knew when
two become a single bolt
the electricity
can reach 100 million volts?
Earth and sky are capacitors
by staying open and willingly close.
With a little too much space
they strike no spark
          and go out.
When connected they grow ecstatic and shout.

## Young and Fast

In used cars and open fields,
in Victorian houses
and downtown hotels,
on stairs or before tall windows,
on midnight drives over mountain ranges
and across the high deserts of eastern Montana
we set ourselves
into each other
as if the collision might
free us from fear
of the loneliness to come.

## Bearhat Dusk

When it came to love,
I didn't know
I had borrowed
a woman
from God,
her parents, and
       herself.

Of her
fears and faults,
the contempt glistening
in our house:
we share crows' feathers
and a field of light.
Dusk. Night.

I love the hem of her dress as
she walks through rooms,
leans against walls,
looks longingly
out windows,
turns
her gaze on me.

Long-fingers tapered
she extends
to the piano,
sets her hands
at rest, plays,
rises, meets me on the couch,
places her feet

in my hands.
When she touches
her hair I remember
morning glories
over the granite ridge of Bearhat Mountain.
The sheer drop to the valley below.

## Montana Lake Sequence

I *East Rosebud Lake*

I've always admired the slant of her
hips in
morning or evening, dawn, midday, dusk,
in light of the fox, the mountain thrush.
In light of all the waxwing daytime midnight love,
in light of her happiness, in light of the sun.

## 2 *Emerald Lake*

With you and me, a certain
subtle but important touching atones
for our frailty
and the unbidden acts of cruelty
we find so difficult to overcome.
Kindness and water, a kiss and laughter,
  the light above your hips and what comes after.

### 3 *Lake At The Falls*

I have my own burdens, I tried
to tell you.
But your burdens,
you said,
burden me.

How can I hear?
God heal
my bones
of familiar lies,

    the bane of men
    the bosom sigh,

the mist and rock
the heavenly eye.

## 4 Mystic Lake

She did look, she said,
closely at another,
a kind of friend
and would be lover
and after the sun
went down
I said with her
shoulders aslant, her arms about her,
I can't blame you
I'm no prize.

I see my shadow
in your dustflower eyes
    making me wonder why we keep
    falling into each other before we sleep.

## She Tells Me To

*for Ariana*

Stop trying to determine
the distance between stars
but see instead our daughter's face
across every expanse:
the unseen but common bridge
of birds and the red contrail of leaves the wind left
below Wolf Mountain, the eyeteeth of bull elk and the sound
thereof in the early dark,
the bear's neck four feet around,
and her strong hands
so good for holding.

## Honeybush

When we meet
at the door,
over the counter,
on the table top,
against the wall
and backlit frontlit
pressed to the glass,
we wonder where
all our anger goes.

## Wilderness

Scaling the face of the Beartooths
beyond the last grip
of roots and shale
wolverines lip the far ridge
and disappear into no man's land.
We go hand over fist,
stand
and look down on Sylvan Lake

and her tail stream,
blue echo of the day.
Bones of an eagle
on the upslant at our feet, wing flare
of longer and shorter bones
we select
and set back one at a time
in their form, carpometacarpus, radius,
and ulna, hand bones
and wing bones,
spine, skull.
At dawn we find ourselves again

in our tent on the skirt
of Sylvan. Light
in the bowl of the earth, light
on your shoulders and hips,
elbows, arms and wrists,
the auburn of your eyes,
jaw and body rise.

# Acknowledgments

With gratitude to editors Christian Wiman, Don Share, Michael Wiegers, Lee Ann Roripaugh, Seabring Davis, Marc Beaudin, Thom Caraway, Jeff Dodd, Keetje Kuipers, Kathleen Flenniken, Allen Jones, Natalie Peeterse, Sharma Shields, Brianna Van Dyke, Ellen Welker, Bill Wetzel and others who first published these poems, sometimes in different forms:

*Big Sky Journal:* "Wilderness"

*Black and White Journal for the Arts:* "This Body"

*The Far Field:* "Between Heaven and Earth"

*Narrative:* "Ecstasy," "Devil's Slide Near Gardner" and "Mountain Homecoming"

*Past Simple:* "Montana Lake Sequence"

*Poetry:* "Hesperus"

*Ruminate:* "Sunrift Gorge, Glacier National Park, Northern Montana: Wife Psalm 2"

*South Dakota Review:* "Dark Horse Bright Field (vii-xxi)"

*Southern Humanities Review:* "Dark Horse Bright Field (i-vi)"

*Poems in Anthologies:*

*Bright Bones: Contemporary Montana Writing:* "Three Forks, Montana, Headwaters of the Missouri," "Sunrift Gorge, Glacier National Park, Montana: Wife Psalm 1 & Wife Psalm 3," "Down from Beartooth Pass," "On Gunsight Mountain" and "Don't Fall"

*Elk River Anthology to Protect Paradise Valley, Montana:* "Radiance, Paradise Valley, The Absaroka-Beartooth Wilderness, Montana" and "Vernal"

*Lilac City Anthology:* "Honeybush"

*Railtown Almanac:* "Three Oceans Plateau, Beartooth Range, Montana"

*Verde Que Te Quiero Verde: After Federico Garcia Lorca:* "Poem for All Who Doubting, Believe" and "Fire of the Body"

"Dark Horse Bright Field" is a sequence of love poems for my wife and a poem in mourning over the Lidice Massacre, near Prague, June 10, 1942.

Thank you to the National Endowment for the Arts for support in the making of these poems.

To C.D. Wright for *Deepstep Come Shining*, Toni Morrison for *Playing in the Dark*, Catherine Barnett for *The Game of Boxes*, Chris Howell for *Love's Last Number*, Li-Young Lee for *The City in Which I Love You*, and Robert Hass for "the woman who dreamed of sunlight."

To Jennifer, my beloved, my friend, the one my soul loves, and to each of our daughters, Natalya, Ariana, and Isabella.

Finally, to the community at Gonzaga University and St. Michael the Archangel Chapel for the ancient prayer, the *Suscipe:* "Take Lord and receive . . ."

SHANN RAY grew up in Montana and Alaska and spent part of his childhood on the Northern Cheyenne reservation. His work has appeared in *Prairie Schooner, Poetry, Esquire, Narrative, Poetry International, McSweeney's, Northwest Review, Big Sky Journal*, and *Salon*. Honors include the American Book Award, a National Endowment for the Arts Creative Writing Fellowship, the High Plains Book Award for poetry, the Bakeless Prize, and the Poetry Quarterly Prize. He is the author of *American Masculine* (Graywolf Press), *Forgiveness and Power in the Age of Atrocity* (Lexington Press), *American Copper* (Unbridled Press), and *Balefire* (Lost Horse Press). A systems psychologist focusing on the psychology of men, he lives in Spokane with his wife and three daughters, and teaches leadership and forgiveness studies at Gonzaga University.